KUSHITES

KUSHITES

In Loving Memory of Toranio and Callington Wallace

MIGUEL BASHFORD

Trendstar Publishing

KUSHITES: In Loving Memory of
Toranio and Callington Wallace

Book cover design by Ruth Hall.
Interior layout by Trendstar Publishing.

Copyright © 2023 Trendstar Publishing.

All rights reserved. No part of this publication may be reproduced, distributed, or transmitted in any form or by any means, including photocopying, recording, or other electronic or mechanical methods, without the prior written permission of the publisher, except in the case of brief quotations embodied in critical reviews and certain other noncommercial uses permitted by copyright law. For permission requests, write to the publisher, addressed "Attention: Permissions Coordinator," at the address below.

Print Book ISBN: 978-1-73752482-3
Ebook ISBN: 978-1-73752483-0

First printing edition 2023.

Trendstar Publishing LLC
2875 S Orange Ave.
Ste: 500-6735
Orlando, Fl, 32806

www.trendstarbooks.com

**THIS IS A
TRUE STORY**

DEDICATION

This book is dedicated to my mother, Paula Hall. Mom, you have always been a queen! I have yet to meet another woman who has been through the struggles and pain that you have survived. You have not allowed obstacles, whether financial issues or physical illness, to break your energy. Your children have watched you maintain your excellent quality over the years. We LOVE you and THANK you for the tremendous effort you put into raising us.

CONTENTS

Text Insert v
Dedication vii

INTRODUCTION 1
1 LIFE IN JAMAICA 5
2 THE CONSTITUTION 11
3 CALLINGTON WALLACE 17
4 TORANIO WALLACE 23
5 THE DAY OF BLOODY MURDER 29
6 THE DAY OF BLOODY MURDER CONTINUED 37
7 NEWS REPORTS 43
8 MORE NEWS REPORTS 49
9 WE NEED JUSTICE 55

EPILOGUE 61
About The Author 65

INTRODUCTION

During the intricate year of 2012, we witnessed many changes, some were universal, and some were in our personal lives. The challenges that most of us faced resulted in a sense of awareness as we entered the new age. The latter part of 2012 was a tragic time for my family, as two of my brothers were murdered, due to police brutality, in the same event. On November 23rd, 2012, in St. Elizabeth, Jamaica, my brothers were killed upon the arrival of a police invasion. This book was written so that I may tell their stories and expose the criminal activities practiced by an organization established to fight crime. When I look closely at the current crisis, I realize that it is a situation that needs to be addressed urgently. The people of Jamaica are being wiped out indiscriminately. No one is safe, not even women or children. The worst part about those murders is that they go without trial or penalty. Roughly 90 percent of all Jamaicans have had someone in their family killed by the police. The level of oppression has caused the citizens to live in terror. However, the police officers are so comfortable with their actions that they may kill a person in the presence of their mother. Then, inform her that her babies will be next when they grow older. In a particular incident, the family of a man who was shot dead was mourning their loss, and when the officer who murdered him noticed, he jeered. "You guys respect this coward? Should have seen how he was begging when I had my gun to his head."

Our mother, Paula Hall, gave birth to five boys. The first two were born one year apart, and then came the middle child two years later, then, two years after him, the last two were also born one year apart. I am the youngest of the five boys, following Paul Bashford Jr., who follows Keron Wallace, the middle child, and then Callington and Toranio Wallace, the first two. Toranio and Callington were the ones who were murdered, and it is because of them that I have composed this manuscript. In December 2000, my brother Paul and I migrated to the U.S. to live with our paternal family. Then, in 2007, our mother, Paula, went on a journey searching for a better way of life. She traveled to the Bahamas, hoping her journey would end in the U.S., where Paul and I lived. Unfortunately, while she was in the Bahamas, our mother was severely beaten and raped by a strange man. Even though she was traumatized, our mother escaped from the evil man and eventually returned to her country, only to find out that she was impregnated from the incident. Then, in July of the year 2008, she gave birth to her first and only daughter, Ruth Hall. My siblings and I were all born and raised in Jamaica, where our mother, a single parent, grew us. She has always been a hardworking woman, and I give her credit for the strength and endurance that she displayed over the years. One of the things that she always told us was that we should not have a need for friends, being that we had enough siblings. As close as my brothers and I were, I admire that we all have unique personalities and separate missions.

If the government of Jamaica wants the people to obey the law, then the government must respect the people's fundamental rights. However, the latter is far from reality, and the citizens share a hatred towards politicians and police officers. Jamaica, where I grew up, was a place to love, and I never imagined that the day would come when I would have to fly from America to bury my brothers. However, my late brothers developed a high level of respect throughout the island while they were alive, and it is safe to say that only heartless police officers could have taken them away so untimely. The incident was the worst tragedy my family has ever faced, and indeed, the sorrow that it caused will last forever.

CHAPTER 1

LIFE IN JAMAICA

Though many may have been corrupted throughout changing times, the beauty of the island remains within the people. Even in a third-world crisis, there are no barriers that can withstand the strength of a family. Unity has preserved my family throughout some devastating times. I spent my childhood in Jamaica up to the time of my adolescence, which was when I migrated to the United States of America. Being an observer, I have noticed the many differences between the environments and the people's lifestyles. Without question, Jamaicans are more vulnerable to violence, hardship, and injustice. Not to say that those miseries do not exist in the U.S., but in America, there are many more opportunities for a person to become successful. There is also much more support to the citizens from the government. For instance, in the United States, besides kindergarten and college, parents do not have to pay for their children to attend grade school. While in Jamaica, parents are required to pay for books and school fees for their children throughout every grade level. There are greater expenses in the island, even though the financial resources are fewer. Typically, there is a price for everything, and that price constantly rises. Nevertheless, Jamaicans love their country, and we share a sense of pride regarding our nationality. However, a common goal among the citizens is to migrate to a place of better opportunities, like America or England, and then later return home after engaging in a better financial situation. That goal is due to the belief that life in those foreign places is much better than the life that they are facing. There is a small percentage of people who attain success without having to leave the island, for instance, entertainers, some business owners, politicians, doctors, and high-level professionals with certain careers. Furthermore, once you attain financial success, you can isolate yourself and find residence in one of the best areas, and then Jamaica may be one of the best places on planet Earth to live. Unfortunately, only a few make it out of the struggle, while the average citizen remains impoverished or dies trying to make it out. The way that the political and economic systems are structured pressures the people to be rather militant minded to survive on a day-to-day basis. Men and women alike must be mentally strong to survive. The economy is not destitute, but the country is indebted to the world powers because of incompetent leadership, which results in hardship for the nation's people. These are people who are mindful of life's finer things but have very few prospects to obtain and enjoy them. The average lifestyle in Jamaica consist of cold showers, stolen or 'bridged' electricity, inadequate plumbing, outdoor charcoal stove cooking, and hand laundry. The chance of getting hired for a long-term, good-paying job of basic labor is quite unusual. Therefore, many people learn certain skill sets or trades, while most acquire independent hustles. Being born and raised in that reality is why most Jamaicans worldwide are usually very handy and hardworking. A place of lesser resources will result in more improvisation from the people. I remember, clear as day, some of the sources of income that my family managed to attain when I was a minor. The closest that we came to a mansion in those days was when my mother did house cleaning for the Azans in their multi million-dollar mansion up in Red Hills. The Azans are an Asian family that owns a chain of retail stores across Jamaica, they are wealthy, and they live like royalty. My mother would take Paul Jr. and I with her some weekends when she went to work there. During most of my childhood, my family's income came from our mother doing what people in Jamaica call 'domestic work,' which is basically housekeeping. As a single parent, she had the task of caring for and providing for five boys. Since she gave birth to all of us when she was rather young, she has spent most of her life dealing with that task. Nevertheless, when my oldest brother Toranio was about 18, he was fortunate enough to get hired at a meat store in Coronation Market. I remember that income was a big help to the family. Most Jamaicans grocery shop at the outdoor markets, which is traditional. Many indoor supermarkets have emerged since my childhood, but every parish's capital still has a big outdoor market. For instance, one in Santa Cruz, St Elizabeth, a market in Spanish Town, St Catherine, one in May Pen, Clarendon, and the most popular one, is in Kingston. The official name for the market in Kingston is Coronation Market, but it is often called 'Downtown,' 'Town,' or 'Dung-Town market.' It is the country's largest outdoor market, and it is surrounded by some of the island's most dangerous garrisons or 'ghettos.' We are talking about places like Tivoli Gardens, Denham Town, Matches Lane, Rema, and Jungle just to name a few. Moreover, the outdoor markets are a big part of Jamaican culture; you can purchase anything there, from clothes and shoes to chicken and fish. The atmosphere in Coronation Market is as follows, heavy traffics of people moving around, including customers, travelers, and vendors with stalls and handcarts advertising their merchandise on top of their voices. Jamaicans eat a lot of ground food, like pumpkins, yams, potatoes, and flour dumplings. Also, the varieties of fruits that the island provides, and vegetables like callaloo and cabbage. You can find all those items at the outdoor markets.

I remember as if it was yesterday that, at one point, my family and I were vendors in Coronation Market under the leadership of our mother. The merchandise that we provided was cooking oil and syrup. After we bought the products in bulk from the wholesale store, we bottled them in smaller containers to make a profit. Then, from there, while our mother stayed at the stall, my brothers and I patrolled the market with a few bottles, shouting at the top of our voices: "Oil! Oil! Syrup!" I laugh now when I reminisce, but I will always cherish my childhood as it made me who I am today.

One of the most significant similarities I have noticed between Jamaica and the United States of America is their constitutions—particularly the people's fundamental rights. For instance, both countries grant freedom of speech and religion and respect for property and life. As there is the concept of due process in the U.S., so are the terms of the Constitution of Jamaica. However, about 70 percent of Jamaican citizens are unaware of these existing laws. One of the main threats that have plagued the citizens over the years is the brutal operations of the Constabulary Force. Procedures that impose fear rather than respect have caused a common hatred between most citizens and the governing system. As it is with most places around the world, the country regions are usually more peaceful than the city areas, and that is the way it once was with Jamaica. For instance, cities like Kingston and Spanish Town were areas where one could expect high crime rates and maybe hear random rounds of ammunition. In the country areas like St Elizabeth or St Mary, it is unlikely to be affected by violence. In those areas, people were usually busy enjoying the rivers, the variety of fruits, farm life, and the overall peace from having to keep up with city life's glamour. Unfortunately, the illegal habits of the Jamaica Constabulary Force (JCF) have brought shame to the most peaceful regions of the island. Citizens are afraid to testify or stand as witness against police officers as there would be grave consequences. They know that they would immediately become a target, victimized, and even tortured if they dared do such a thing. Therefore, countless cruelty situations go without trial or any form of justice. However, I choose to be one of the few to use my voice as an instrument, to cry out for justice, and to let the listening ear hear my family's pain. Also, I hope to inspire every Jamaican citizen to study and learn the laws of the Constitution so that we may stand together for our rights instead of continually surrendering them.

CHAPTER 2

THE CONSTITUTION

The Constitution of Jamaica was established on July 23, 1962. Before that, the island was a British colony, which was governed directly from Britain. On August 6, 1962, Jamaica became an independent country, even though it remained a member of the British Commonwealth. A Constitution consists of the fundamental laws on which a nation is established, it determines the powers and duties of the government and guarantees certain rights to the people. It is essential to the existence and functionality of any civilized nation. Therefore, for a country to function properly, the citizens including government officials must respect and obey the regulations of the Constitution. Only then will that nation stand firm and sustain independence. The documents that you are about to review are extracts from the official Constitution of Jamaica, and they are copied and pasted in this book for information purposes only. Document 1 is the first draft of the Constitution from 1962, and Document 2 is the updated version from 2011. The most critical section of the Constitution for Jamaican citizens in my opinion is Chapter 3, because it deals with the people's fundamental rights. I will only present the Chapter's portion that is relevant to the current crisis.

Nevertheless, I strongly advise every Jamaican to take the time to study and be knowledgeable of the Constitution in its entirety.

DOCUMENT_1:

At the Court at Buckingham Palace, the 23rd day of July 1962
Present,
THE QUEEN'S MOST EXCELLENT MAJESTY IN COUNCIL

Chapter III
Fundamental Rights and Freedoms

Whereas every person in Jamaica is entitled to the fundamental rights and freedoms of the individual, that is to say, he has the right, whatever his race, place of origin, political opinions, color, creed, or sex, but subject to respect for the rights and freedoms of others and for the public interest, to each and all of the following, namely-

life, liberty, security of the person, the enjoyment of property, and the protection of the law;

freedom of conscience, of expression, and of peaceful assembly and association; and

respect for his private and family life, the subsequent provisions of this Chapter shall have effect for the purpose of affording protection to the aforesaid rights and freedoms, subject to such limitations of that protection as are contained in those provisions being limitations designed to ensure that the enjoyment of the said rights and freedoms by any individual does not prejudice the rights and freedoms of others or the public interest.

(1) No person shall intentionally be deprived of his life save in execution of the sentence of a court in respect of a criminal offense of which he has been convicted.

(2) Without prejudice to any liability for a contravention of any other law with respect to the use of force in such cases as are hereinafter mentioned, a person shall not be regarded as having been deprived of his life in contravention of this section if he dies as the result of the use of force to such extent as is reasonably justifiable in the circumstances of the case -
for the defense of any person from violence or for the defense of property; in order to effect a lawful arrest or to prevent the escape of a person lawfully detained; for the purpose of suppressing a riot, insurrection, or mutiny; or in order lawfully to prevent the commission by that person of a criminal offense, or if he dies as the result of a lawful act of war.

(1) No person shall be subjected to torture or to inhuman or degrading punishment or other treatment.

1) Except with his own consent, no person shall be subject to the search of his person or his property or the entry by others on his premises.

1) Except with his own consent, no person shall be hindered in the enjoyment of his freedom of conscience, and for the purposes of this section, the said freedom includes freedom of thought and of religion, freedom to change his religion or belief, and freedom, either alone or in community with others, and both in public and in private, to manifest and propagate his religion or belief in worship, teaching, practice, and observance.

DOCUMENT_2:

The Charter of Fundamental Rights and freedoms (Constitutional Amendment) Act, 2011

(3) The rights and freedoms referred to in subsection (2) are as follows

(a) the right to life, liberty, and security of the person and the right not to be deprived thereof except in the execution of the sentence of a court in respect of a criminal offence of which the person has been convicted;

(b) the right to freedom of thought, conscience, belief, and observance of political doctrines;

(c) the right to freedom of expression;

(d) the right to seek, receive, distribute or disseminate information, opinions and ideas through any media;

(g) the right to equality before the law;

(h) the right to equitable and humane treatment by any public authority in the exercise of any function;

(i) the right to freedom from discrimination
on the ground of

(i) being male or female;

(ii) race, place of origin, social
class, color, religion or
political opinions;

(j) the right of everyone to

(i) protection from search of the
person and property;

(ii) respect for and protection of
private and family life, and
privacy of the home; and

(ill) protection of privacy of other
property and of communication;

(1) the right to enjoy a healthy and productive
environment free from the threat of injury
or damage from environmental abuse and
degradation of the ecological heritage;

Under our Common Law system, all citizens of whatever rank or status are subject to the same set of laws, and the exercise of governmental power is limited by those laws. The Supreme Court is empowered to review legislation but only to determine whether it conforms to constitutional requirements.

THE END.

The JCF is an organization that was ordained by this same Constitution. Upon the foundation of those terms, Jamaica was granted its independence. Sadly, those laws are well forgotten a little over fifty years later. It is now a regular thing to witness a person being tortured, and government officials are usually the ones doing the torture. Inhumane treatment from police officers can be expected on any random contact. Crime and violence are worldwide issues, but those actions are unbearable when law enforcers are the ones committing them. For Jamaicans to have peace and a sustainable future, everyone must return their focus back to the terms of the Constitution

CHAPTER 3

CALLINGTON WALLACE

He was born on March 29th, 1981, in Clarendon, Jamaica, to Ms. Paula Hall and Mr. Baston Wallace. Callington Wallace was also known as Carl, Busky, or Busky Bash. He grew up throughout the parishes of Clarendon, St Elizabeth, and St Catherine, and ever since he was a child, he had been introduced to a life of poverty. Moreover, the struggle was a circumstance to which he early adapted. At an early age, he displayed high ambition, self esteem, and confidence. Carl was already seven years old when I was born, and it is safe to say that all his younger siblings were privileged to have him as a big brother. For us, our big brothers were the examples of our future maturity. Callington was overprotective regarding his family, especially his little brothers, and there have been incidents when he had to maltreat older guys in our defense. He was always there for us as a guide throughout our childhood endeavors. Two years before I was born, when Carl was only five years old, he survived a terrible accident. One day, in Clarendon, he was trying to cross a highway street by himself and was hit by a speeding truck. Carl was in critical condition and had to stay in Acoma for weeks. Many people lost hope of his survival when they saw how severely injured he was, , but not our mother. She has always been a prayer warrior and a firm believer. Callington made it out of that hospital after about a month of recovery, with good health, strength, and flexibility. He still had some huge scars on his head and across his body that he had to live with for the rest of his life, and that is how I met him. I am grateful that he survived that accident because it gave me a chance to know him. Carl had been enduring pain since he was young, and it made him grow with the mentality of a survivor and a warrior. When I was nine years old, I also found myself in a condition of serious injury from an accident that caused a severe brain concussion. Again, our mother was there with her faith and positivity throughout the entire situation. I am fortunate to be alive and well today, with the strength to expose the evil that was done to my brothers. I believe that the survival of those accidents fueled a fire inside of me and in Carl.

Callington's drive and his hustle would outdo any other; he was literally always on the move. He dedicated his focus to escaping poverty. Indeed, he was a trying youth. It was improbable to find him engaging in gossip or idle gesturing because there was always a task that captured his attention. He was ambitious and independent.

Out of my mother's five sons, he is the one with the most charisma. Carl had an irresistible connection with women. I had never seen him fail in that area. Even today, some of the lines Junior and I use on women came straight from his catalog. After he was murdered and I traveled to Jamaica, I spoke with a few people that knew him well. Everyone attested to his militancy, his drive, and his ambition. Portmore, St Catherine, was one of the places where he left his stamp, and in that area, all the talk was about Busky Bash.

One of his peers from Portmore quoted: "Yow, a hunt dem man deh use to hunt streets!"

Someone else said. "When dem man deh come round', the bar never lock!"

One of the females in the area mentioned that she would give him anything whenever he was in need because he was the one usually on the giving end.

Another female joked about how Carl would show up to crash at her house on random nights, and he would sometimes have a friend or two with him, but she never turned him down. He was a sojourner.

Indeed he was a mighty warrior, and he upheld the mindset of a boss. He would not violate anyone else's property but he would protect his own with a vengeance. He was passionate about his mission in life and his role as a provider. Moreover, there was a side of him that was very affectionate.

One day, when Junior and I were about 7 and 8 years old, we had just returned to the neighborhood from school, Carl met us on the block, and we tried to greet him handshakes. However, he turned down the handshakes and greeted us with hugs and kisses on our foreheads. It was awkward, but we knew our big brother was genuine.

A person living in Jamaica's society is faced with an ultimatum to be a victim or a conqueror. Callington chose to be a conqueror, a predator, instead of a prey. He met his girlfriend Tamara Thomas in his late teens, and then a few years later when he was twenty-one years old, they gave birth to a beautiful daughter, Pretanya Wallace. That was in the year 2002. His daughter added to his motivation, and to his reasons for acquiring millions of dollars. Two years after Pretanya was born, Carl launched his cash-for-gold business. I remember talking to him on the phone while I was here in America and him telling me to find him a decent gold testing machine. In the cash-for-gold business is where Carl was most successful compared to all the other efforts he made to make an income. A few years into the business, he was already approaching the top level, earning hundreds of thousands of Jamaican dollars. His goal was to open a brick-and-mortar store that buys and sells gold.

Unfortunately, during the vulnerable rise of his business, Carl was robbed twice. On both occasions, he was wounded to the point where he almost lost his life. He suffered significant financial losses from those robberies. The first incident was carried out by gunmen who watched and followed him until he was alone in a remote area. They caught him one night over by Hellshire Beach and beat him badly, and then they took everything he had; they almost killed him. The second incident was carried out by police officers during a random traffic stop in Spanish Town, St Catherine. The officers confiscated his money, which amounted to about three thousand U.S. dollars, and his jewelry which was worth more than the cash he was carrying. On top of that, they broke a few of his fingers and left him on the scene severely beaten and wounded. I will explain later how this second robbery was directly connected to the brutal execution of my brothers. Callington was murdered at the tender age of 31 while he was still in pursuit of happiness. His daughter was only 10 years old when he passed, and she was left without a father. He is yet another precious life stripped away by ruthless members of the Jamaica Constabulary Force.

To: Callington

"I will always salute you, my big brother. I pray you reign in peace!!"

CHAPTER 4

TORANIO WALLACE

Toranio Wallace was born on January 23, 1980, in Clarendon, Jamaica, as the first child of Ms. Paula Hall and Mr. Baston Wallace. He grew up in the parishes of Clarendon, St Catherine, and St Elizabeth where his father lived. Toranio was better known as Shortman, Pedro, Taz, or Kush. Our mother always tells the story of how Kush was born, he entered the world prematurely at about seven months, and she said that he came out of her womb completely wrapped in white slime. The doctors had to use scissors to cut the slime off his body. She acknowledged that it was an unusual birth and that only prophets were born in such a condition. Furthermore, it was clear throughout his life that Kush was a chosen seed. Mom always talk about how helpful he was to her. When he was as little as six years old, he was going to the market by himself for our mother, and he took on many more responsibilities to help her out, like helping with us his younger siblings when we came into the world.

People loved to be in his presence because of his positive vibes. Compared to all my mother's children, Kush was the humblest and the craftiest. His style was unique and outstanding, the most fashionable of all. He mastered the art of dancing, which is a huge part of Jamaican culture. Naturally, like the famous Bogle, a Jamaican dancer, Kush was smooth and his moves were impeccable. He was about 5 feet and 7 inches tall, the oldest and the shortest of the brothers. Nevertheless, he was the neatest, and his personality was the most collected. It was a great experience to grow up with Kush as a big brother. His love for his family was unconditional.

Moreover, he was a seeker of knowledge and he acquired a great deal of it throughout his lifetime. Therefore, he was well-versed in matters of history, religion, and some political affairs. He came to the realization that he was a descendant of Kushites, who were people from the Kingdom of Kush, which is now known as Nubia in Africa. Henceforth, he took on the name Kush, which led me to name this book Kushites. His knowledge and love for teaching caused me, Junior, and Keron to be aware of certain secrets of the world since we were minors. He was a great teacher, and we were his first students. The best days of my life were when we all lived under the same roof in Portmore, St Catherine. It was Ms. Paula and her five boys since our little sister, Ruth, was not yet born. I remember Kush would gather Junior and me some nights after dinner, and we would reason for hours. We would explore topics like the different world powers, including the Eagle, the Dragon, and the Bear, and what they represent. It was important to him to share all the information he had gathered with us, and outside of Christianity, I give him full credit for being the source of our early awareness. Kush was my big brother and my teacher. I respect the very ground that he walked on! He was deeply in tune with his roots and he was very cultural. A nurturer at heart, and his intentions were always pure. People outside of his family loved his vibes once they met him, and he connected with the youths because he was most patient, and he embraced them. Kush quickly became our little sister's favorite big brother once she was born. Moreover, he was even closer to our mother than he was to us, his siblings. He was the one that she was always able to count on.

In a soft tone, our mother once said. "No one can I compare to Shortman. He was my tender child."

Kush would never initiate conflict, he was not the type to quarrel or strife with anyone. At the same time, he was far from a pushover and he wouldn't hesitate to get aggressive when it was necessary, quite similar to a roaring lion. Naturally he was a humanitarian, a peacemaker, even in the rogue structure of Jamaica's society. When he was 21 years old, he met Melisa Bailey, and the following year they gave birth to their only son, Dayshawn Wallace. While Dayshawn was growing up, his father was still on the mission of securing a better future for his family. Around that time, Kush had gotten the opportunity to travel to the Cayman Islands for an employment visit. Therefore, he went there and worked for a while, and then when the permit expired he returned home to Jamaica. When he returned, he had an even greater interest in the knowledge of self. Unlike Busky, who dedicated most of his time to ensuring financial security, Kush was less concerned with the cares of the world and more concerned with his spiritual development. He kept a wide variety of books, and as he grew he got deeper into his studies. It is safe to say that Kush had reached the heights and the depths of understanding. People who loved and respected him stretched to many areas across the island, but his best impressions were with the people in Kingston.

A young man in Kingston whom I spoke to shared his comments about Kush. "When dem man deh come round', he associates with the people. That means we playing dominoes, and running boats!"

The phrase 'run a boat' means to have a group of people, two or more, decide on a meal to cook, then everyone who are involved contributes to providing the food and the other ingredients that are needed. Then, after that the best chef in the group would do the cooking, and when it is done everyone would eat and enjoy.

Unlike Busky Bash who was always on the move and barely found time for leisure, whenever Kush was in the area, he might sometimes be spotted reasoning with the elders, or even playing football with the youths. Everyone loved when he came around, because the place would be full of good vibes.

The scriptures state, "if you live by the gun, you will die by the gun." Well, Kush did not live by the gun, yet he was assassinated by uniformed gunmen. To earn money, he often performed masonry labor, and sometimes he held Fish Fries, where he cooked, and the community supported him. He never got himself involved in criminal activities. However, at the young age of 32, crooked police officers shot Kush down in cold blood. In that event, he was still dressed in his work clothes after he had just finished an honest day of work. His death was absolute martyrdom! With the voice of my family along with everyone else who knew him, we say sincerely: 'What a wonderful son, brother, friend, and warrior we have lost!'

To: Kush

"For this cause, my brother, justice will come.
May you reign in peace forever!"

CHAPTER 5

THE DAY OF BLOODY MURDER

Friday, November 23rd, 2012 was the bloody day. It was Black Friday in America, the day after Thanksgiving Day . The time was between 3 and 4 pm. I was at home in Miami, Florida, on the veranda playing dominoes with a friend when I got the news. My brother Junior came walking back from the corner-store, and as he got closer, I noticed a disgusted look on his face, immediately I sensed that something was wrong.

He had gotten a phone call from Jamaica with the devastating news as he was walking back from the corner-store. When he made it to where we were sitting, he said to me bitterly. "Yow, Miguel, police just killed Busky!"

I was speechless when I heard it, and I threw my hand of dominoes on the table and stood up. Words cannot explain the adrenaline rush or the thoughts that ran through my head. It was mind-blowing!

"Bombo-Claawt, bredda! Weh yuh jus seh?"

As we fell apart emotionally, Junior's phone rang, and again it was another call from Jamaica. The caller was the same person who had called a few minutes earlier to inform us of Callington's death. It was a friend of my brothers in Jamaica and he was calling in the event of the tragedy. I was able to hear the chaos in the caller's background as he spoke loudly and disturbingly to us.

"Yow, Junior Bash, dem kill Shortman too, dawg!" said the caller.

"What?! Dem kill Shortman too?" Junior asked the caller. "Blood-Clawt! So, where is Pome?" he continued. Pome is the nickname of Keron Wallace, our mother's third born son.

"Yow, family, him can't talk right now. Him inna the middle of the street pon him knees a wol Shortman inna him hands and a bawl! Dem covered in blood. Pome a lose it right now!" The caller replied.

It wasn't much said after that, and Junior eventually hung up the phone miserably. As our world rapidly crumbled, we both experienced a loss for words. Momentarily, I went inside the house, powered on my laptop, and booked a one-way ticket to Kingston, Jamaica. I was to arrive in Kingston that following Tuesday.

Returning to my home country was a bittersweet experience. Joy and sorrow were in the atmosphere simultaneously. After all, Junior and I had been gone for 12 years, meaning it had been 12 long years since we saw our mother and brothers in person. We were unable to return to Jamaica throughout that period of time because of naturalization issues. However, it so happened that my residential status upgraded earlier that same year, just a couple of months before the tragedy occurred. In August of 2012, I finally received my permanent resident card, allowing me to travel back and forth overseas without penalty. I was already planning to take my first trip back home, the right way, the upcoming Christmas holiday of that year. Unfortunately, I had to make that emergency visit in November. Sadly, Junior was not able to travel with me because his naturalization process was not yet completed. Nevertheless, I am thankful that, at least, I was able to go. A common dream among my brothers and our mother was that we would all reunite one day and live together like we did in Portmore. The last time I saw my big brothers in person, they were still teenagers, except for Kush, who was 20.

Even though it was not the reunion that we imagined, I was still glad to reunite with mommy and Pome and to meet our little sister, Ruth, for the first time in person. Ruth was four years old at that time. The purpose of my return was to assist in the burial of my beloved brothers, and to be a strength emotionally to our mother who was weakened from the experience. Overall, it was heartbreaking to say the least. Moreover, I reunited with Pome, and he told me all about the day of the bloody murder.

"Bredda, if it wasn't for my urge to go get a drink that day, right now me wouldah be a dead man too," said Pome.

The bloody day began like any other regular day. Kush had finished his day's work early that afternoon, and he and my other two brothers met at their father's house.

Most Jamaicans have some family members who live in the country parishes and some living in the city parishes, causing them to travel back and forth regularly. So it was with my brothers, they were never in one parish for an entire year, being that their father lived in St. Elizabeth and our mother was living in Kingston at the time. Therefore, they would spend a few months in Town and then a few months in the countryside whenever they were ready to cool out. On the day of the bloody murder, all three of them were together in the countryside of Black River, St Elizabeth.

    Pome told me that when him, Shortman, and Busky linked up that day, they were just relaxing in their father's backyard, reasoning, as they all smoked the same spliff. There were no business agendas planned for the rest of the day, they were just chilling. Everything was going smoothly until they came upon a slight disagreement in their conversation, which they usually did. Eventually, the debate led Pome to leave Shortman and Busky and walk to the store to get a drink. He wanted something strong so he went to the liquor store. The time it took him to walk from their father's house to the liquor store, was approximately 20 minutes each way. There were closer stores or 'shops' within the neighborhood, but Pome decided to walk down to the entrance of the community to the main store. Within that 40 to 60 minute window while Pome was gone, was when the tragedy unfolded.

    The invasion went as follows: Four undercover police officers, three men, and a woman, entered the neighborhood driving a taxicab. They parked up the block from my brothers' father, Baston Wallace's home. Then, they got out of the cab, dressed in regular clothing as if they were civilians. However, their guns were drawn as they maneuvered. Simultaneously, a van pulled up and parked on the adjacent block which was behind Mr. Baston's house. That van was filled with police officers wearing blue denim overalls, carrying high-powered rifles. Two of the officers who arrived in the taxicab approached the house from the front street, while the other two went towards it from the backyard area. People who first noticed them were disturbed because they did not recognize the strangers. Those police officers were from a different jurisdiction.

As the assassins approached, Kush was chilling in the neighbor's backyard, next to his father's house. Callington had just walked to the shop, which was right up the block, and Mr. Baston Wallace was outside in his yard doing some mechanical work. Mr. Baston was shocked when the intruders jumped the fence into his yard, and he questioned them immediately.

"Hey, what you strange men doing in I man yard?" he asked disturbingly.

One of the assassins quickly pointed his gun at Mr. Baston and yelled. "Shut the fuck up before I blow out your brains!"

Then, they spotted Kush in the next yard and attacked him immediately. Without hesitation, one of them fired and shot Kush in the area of his rib-cage.

Mr. Baston Wallace cried out for his son as he watched, dreading the fact that there was nothing he could have done at the moment. Callington was now returning from the shop to the yard where he had left his brother, Kush. Therefore, as soon as he turned the corner towards the yard, that was when he heard the gunshot that went into Kush's ribs. Carl noticed the strange men from a distance, as they were harassing his brother. The murderers looked up and caught a glimpse of Carl, then immediately, they went after him with open fire. Kush was left to suffer and bleed out.

When Callington recognized the faces of the strange men, he was appalled, and he whispered to himself as he took off running. "Damn! These are the same police boys dem' who robbed me in Spanish Town!"

Now, this is where the dots were connected. There were two main reasons why those officers carried out the brutal operation. The first one was because of a guy named Guns who they had busted back in the year 2007, because of his involvement in a drug for guns trade with Haiti. Undercover police officers had been secretly watching Guns since he was released from prison. Guns was from New Town, the same neighborhood as my brothers, and they all knew each other. However, without any proof or evidence, the officers assumed that anyone who associated with Guns were a part of the ongoing trade. Furthermore, instead of arresting the suspects and giving them a fair trial, those officers were only concerned with shooting to kill. The second reason that fueled the operation was a court case in 2012 that was nearly approaching a verdict. It was my brother Callington Wallace vs. the police officers who had beaten and robbed him in Spanish Town. After that incident, Carl hired a lawyer and took the situation to court. He was attempting to sue those crooked cops, and rightfully, the case was leaning in his favor. A severe penalty was in the future of those unlawful men. They were going to have to return all of Callington's possessions - his money and his jewelry, reimburse him for the treatment costs of his injuries, face dismissal from office, and possibly serve time in jail.

Carl was practically playing with fire, because in Jamaica, it is profoundly dangerous to threaten an officer about losing his or her position. Whenever those situations arise, the officers quickly take action by murdering everything that stands against them.

Therefore, it was a top priority for those killer cops from Spanish Town to murder not only Callington, but all three of the Wallace brothers. So, when they learned of the upcoming operation in New Town, St. Elizabeth, they gladly voluntared to take on the front line. Then, my brothers' neighborhood was invaded less than two weeks before the trial of that lawsuit.

CHAPTER 6

THE DAY OF BLOODY MURDER CONTINUED

Callington took off running, around the corner towards the street. The other two officers who were approaching the house from the front noticed the action, and instantly, they assisted their comrades in the pursuit. Therefore, all four of the assassins were now shooting at Carl. He came running full speed around the corner, and he managed to slip through the intersecting attacks as he made his way up the block. Unfortunately, he was already hit once or twice during that maneuver. However, he was still going. Then, the four shooters lined up side by side horizontally in the middle of the street, and together they fired, sending hundreds of rounds of ammunition up the block towards Callington. My brother ran desperately for his life as bullets came at him from all angles. The killers were firing wildly in the open street, gunning at my brother with a thirst for blood. Not long after, Callington collapsed on the sidewalk up the block, about forty yards away from where the killers lined up. He was shot seven times and he died right there on the spot.

These actions were unfolding in broad daylight, in the eyes of many civilians, including children, some of whom were just arriving home from school that day. The next victim of the deadly operation was a young man who was leaving the same shop that Carl had visited a few minutes earlier. He was just heading down the block when he saw Busky running and the killers firing a barrage of bullets. Before the young man was able to find cover, he was also gunned down in the middle of the street by those murderers. On the adjacent block behind Mr Baston's house, the police officers who were wearing blue denim overalls spotted Kenrick Bennett, otherwise known as Guns. They jumped out of the van immediately and started shooting at Guns. They did not cease fire until they were certain that they had killed him. The residents of that peaceful community were traumatized, as no such incident had ever came close to that area, the place is rather small and everyone pretty much know each other. Therefore, weeping and mourning was heard loudly as the brutality unfolded.

After Guns was killed, the murderers came together and stacked the three dead bodies on the back of a small pickup truck and carried them away. Kush was still in the backyard fighting to stay alive. He placed his hands on his side where he was wounded, attempting to slow down the blood flow. Then, he stumbled and crawled towards some banana trees that are in the yard, as he tried to hide himself amongst them.

At that time, one of the killers who were still on the scene was patrolling the block with his rifle, checking from yard to yard to ensure that there were no survivors. When he got to the yard where Kush was located, he noticed the blood trail that led to the banana trees, so he followed it. My brother was found with his hands on his ribs, trying to hide between two banana trees. Then, the dirty cop dragged him back out in the open and told him to lie down on his face. Momentarily, the murderer commanded Kush to get on his knees and put his hands behind his head as he held him at gunpoint. Kush did as he was told.

"Hey bwoy, which part the guns dem deh?" The killer cop asked.

"Which guns, officer? Nuh unuh bring all the guns dem to come kill us off?!" Kush replied with annoyance. "Yuh friends dem shot me already, and now you come to shoot me again?!"

"Bwoy, shut the fuck up! And open your mouth," said the killer, as he shoved his rifle into Kush's mouth.

Then, seconds later, the trigger happy policeman squeezed the trigger and blew my brother's brains through the back of his head. When he looked up, he saw a woman watching. It was my brother's Aunt, she was watching and crying from outside the gate.

Immediately, the so called officer of the law swung his rifle in her direction and yelled. "Hey, big pussy gal, run back inna yuh yard, before me slap a shot inna your face!"

The lady was terrified and she fled without hesitation. Then, the murderer continued to drag Kush's dead body to the front of the house, out in the street amid the uproar.

One of the news crews had arrived just in time to catch that part on camera. Therefore, there is a published news clip in the media that shows the officer dragging Kush's dead body from the backyard.

At that time, Pome was just returning to the area with his drink and chaser. Nevertheless, he had heard the last few gunshots from a distance, and he knew that something was wrong. Therefore, he began to run back to his block. The noise increased as he got closer, and Pome realized that there was chaos in his neighborhood. Insecurity and instability kicked in, as his mind wondered. Then, he was met en-route by one of his friends, who delivered the terrible news to him that Callington was murdered. Pome couldn't believe it, but he told his friend to call me and Junior and let us know what was going on, as he continued towards his father's house. It was at that time when Junior received the first phone call about the tragic news.

When Pome finally arrived at the scene, Busky was already taken away, and he found Kush lying lifeless in the street, leaking blood. Keron had an emotional breakdown when he saw what those evil cops had done to his brother. He cried and screamed at the top of his lungs as he knelt in the street with Kush in his hands, covered in blood. It was at that time when Junior received the second phone call, the one for which I was present.

As Pome and I were catching up, I asked him. "Were there any last words from Kush?"

He replied. "No, bro. Me call, and call. Me seh, Shortman! Shortman! Talk to me, bredda!, Talk to me, please! Me don't get no answer.... just see blood a run from him mouth."

Shortman and Busky were dead before Pome returned to the block. For him it was a traumatic experience, especially that he realized he would have been dead as well if he had not gone for a drink.

From my observation, mentally, Keron has not been the same since that bloody day.

Somehow, the bloodthirsty murderers were unsatisfied. They later reported that their mission was to kill at least six people, including the 3 Wallace brothers. I can't help but consider that maybe I would be dead as well if I had flown to Jamaica about a week before November 23, being that more than likely, I would have been right there with my big brothers. My family has suffered greatly from this tragedy, especially our mother. However, I am aware that we have only added to the archives of families who have suffered from the same corruption.

CHAPTER 7

NEWS REPORTS

I have gathered the news reports of five different reporters that had coverage of the incident. These reports are copied and pasted from their sources which are the top news broadcasters in Jamaica, including the Gleaner, the Observer, and others. They are presented here exactly how they were published. Therefore, please note that there will be many errors and contradictions throughout them, for instance, incorrect name spellings, incorrect dates, and misinformation about the overall operation. Moreover, there are some essential facts in the context of the reports, confirming some of the information that has been written in the previous chapters. I will share my comments after each report to make corrections, highlight specific phrases, and clarify misunderstandings.

REPORT 1

The police are yet to provide details of an incident in which 4 men were shot dead by cops in New Town St. Elizabeth yesterday (November 23). However, a statement this afternoon (November 24) from the Police High Command says the men were involved in the drugs for guns trade. The dead men have been identified as Rohan Barrett of Tivoli Gardens in Kingston; as well as Kenrick Bennett otherwise called Guns, of Parottee; along with brothers Carlington and Turine Wallace, both of New Town, all from St. Elizabeth. Police say two 9 millimetre pistols and seven rounds of ammunition were seized in the incident.

The statement from the Jamaica Constabulary Force (JCF) says Kenrick Bennett along with other men were detained by Cuban authorities on July 5, 2007. This after they were caught in Cuban waters with seven 9 millimetre pistols, three revolvers and 1,170 rounds of ammunition.

The men were reportedly returning from Haiti where they had gone to trade 2,000 pounds of marijuana for weapons and ammunition.

Police say Bennett and the other men were subsequently returned to Jamaica and all were charged with conspiracy to transport firearms to Jamaica and conspiracy to export marijuana.

The case was adjourned sine die as the main prosecution witness could not be found to give testimony. The police say they strongly believe that Bennett, Barrett and the two Wallace brothers were involved in the guns for drug trade with Haiti. Last night, police told Irie FM News that the men were killed in a shootout, but gave no details. However, residents reported hearing a barrage of gunshots in the area, about 4:30 p.m. They say shortly after, some men were observed running in different directions. The residents also claim that they observed men dressed in blue denim overall, believed to be police officers. They say when the shooting subsided, three men were found suffering from gunshot wounds.

The wounded men were taken to the Black River Hospital by the police. About half an hour later, residents reportedly stumbled upon the body of the fourth victim and called the black river police. All 4 men were pronounced dead at hospital.

The fatal shootings have been reported to the Independent Commission of Investigations (Indecom).

MY COMMENTS

The first error in this report is the spelling of my brothers' names, which should be Callington and Toranio instead of Carlington and Turine. Then, the report states that two 9-millimeter pistols were seized in the incident. Well, four men were killed in three different locations, so there should be more clarity on who possessed those firearms, if the above statement was even true. Furthermore, the second and third paragraphs of this report had nothing whatsoever to do with my brothers. The JCF brought up a case involving Kenrick Bennett, a.k.a Guns, which happened five years before this invasion. The police officers were trying to frame my brothers with the allegations in attempt to justify their acts of cruelty. The report states: "The police say they strongly believe..." Was that enough for them to kill someone? Where is the proof? Those crooked cops even had the audacity to tell Irie Fm that the victims were killed in a shootout. Nevertheless, the entire community can bare witnesses that no one else was shooting besides those invaders. A couple things that this report did confirm, was that there were men wearing blue denim overalls and that the fourth victim, which was Kush, was found last. However, it states that the fourth victim was first seen by the residents, but the truth is, Kush was discovered by one of the murderers while he was still alive. Lastly, the report states that the men were pronounced dead at the hospital, but in reality, they all died on the scene.

REPORT 2

Two brothers among 4 killed by Police in St. Elizabeth

As details surface on yesterday's fatal shooting of four men in the community of New Town, Black River, St. Elizabeth, it has been revealed that two of the men killed were brothers who are only known by their aliases, 'Pedro' and 'Carlington', however the full identities of the men have yet to be revealed.

Details surrounding the fatal shooting of the men have yet to be released by the Police, however unconfirmed reports are that the men were conducting mason work on a premises in the New Town community when the incident took place.

MY COMMENTS

For the most part, this report was based on my brothers, Shortman and Busky. It is confirmed here that they were conducting mason work in the community that same day. They were making an honest living.

REPORT 3
(Jamaica Observer)

Police kill four men in St Elizabeth
Friday, November 23, 2012

...When contacted, Director of Communications for the Jamaica constabulary, Karl Angell confirmed the incident but said he could give no further details, as he had not yet been briefed.

Angell said that, "as is the normal situation in cases like these the matter has been reported to the Independent Commission of Investigations (INDECOM)."

"Dem a nuh wrong doer," a young woman who claimed to know the four men, told the Observer.

She alleged that the police party had come from outside the parish.

Police sources suggested that at least two of the men were suspected to have been involved in the 'drugs for guns' trade.

MY COMMENTS

This report is one of the most important ones. I would imagine that the Director of Communications for the Jamaica Constabulary Force, Karl Angel, would be aware of an operation of such magnitude, even long before it was carried out. However, it is stated here that he was not aware, and that is only because it was a private operation, those officers who did the dirt, were operating with their own ulterior motives. The victims were being treated like they were wild animals. Furthermore, if they were all criminals, then the residents of that community would have been at peace. Instead, if you watch any of the live footage, you would see that the residents were facing much agony as they mourned their losses. They cried as if it was their own sons that were murdered. The woman the reporter interviewed served as a voice of the community who knew my brothers well, and she confirmed that they were "no wrongdoers," in other words, they were not criminals. The woman also confirmed that the assassins came from outside the parish, and from the information that we have already gathered, we know that they were from Spanish Town. The last sentence of this report states, "The police suggested that it was at least two of the victims who were suspected of being involved in the drugs for guns trade." Well, if that was the case, why were four men murdered?

CHAPTER 8

MORE NEWS REPORTS

REPORT 4

Member of Parliament for Southwest St. Elizabeth the ruling People's National Party (PNP), Hugh Buchanan has called for a speedy investigation into Friday's incident in the community of New Town in the southern Parish which four men were killed during a reported confrontation with the police. Residents contend that the men were chased and shot by the police. It's reported that two brothers were among those killed in what was said to be an operation involving police stationed outside of the Parish. In condemning the shooting, Mr. Buchanan condemned the incident.

He has also demanded answers as to whether any guns, ammunition or any contraband was seized following the shooting.

The Southwest St. Elizabeth Member of parliament expressed support for the police in their efforts to minimize incidents of major crime and violence.

Meanwhile, Mr. Buchanan has urged residents to be on the lookout for criminals who have sought haven in sections of St. Elizabeth.

Those killed have been identified as Carlton Wallace ,31, his brother Teranio, 33 and Kendrick Bennett - all three are from St. Elizabeth. The fourth victim has been identified as Rohan Warren of Tivoli Gardens in Kingston.

According to reports, shortly after 3pm on Friday, a police team converged on a section of the New Town Housing scheme following which residents heard explosions.

The bodies of four men, with what appeared to be gunshot wounds, were found lying in three different locations.

MY COMMENTS

It is stated in this report that the men had confrontation with the police, but that is not true, the victims were all caught unaware in vulnerable positions at the time of the invasion. I am uncertain about the other two men, but sources confirmed that no drugs nor guns were found in either of my brothers' possessions. The residents of that community are eyewitnesses of the manner in which the killers from Spanish Town sought after Callington, it was as if he was a stray dog. Note, it is stated that Member of Parliament, Hugh Buchanan, condemned the incident. However, Mr. Buchanan should realize that the criminals who the residents should be on the lookout for are people like those undercover police officers. My brothers grew up in that neighborhood, so everyone knew them and loved them. To this day they still have family members living in New Town. Again, my brothers' names were misspelled in this report, and their ages are incorrect. They were 31 and 32 years old when they were murdered. Nevertheless, this report did confirm that the bodies of the victims were found in three different locations.

REPORT 5
(Jamaica Observer)

Four killed in St Elizabeth
were linked to gun trade, say cops
Sunday, November 25, 2012

PUBLIC anger continued to smoulder in St Elizabeth yesterday at the shooting deaths of four men by the police in the community of New Town, just outside the parish capital Black River mid-afternoon Friday.

The residents are alleging that the men were killed in cold blood and that the police fired indiscriminately during the incident which happened between 3:00 pm and 4:00 pm when students were on their way home from school.

"Shots were being fired wildly and anybody could have been hit," said Councillor Mordant Mitchell (PNP, Black River Division). People in the community, he said, were traumatised.

Yesterday, police identified the four men as Kenrick Bennett of Parottee, St Elizabeth; Rohan Barrett of Tivoli Gardens, Kingston; Carlington Wallace; and Turine Wallace of New Town.

Police said that two 9mm pistols and seven rounds of ammunition were seized at the scene.

At least two of the dead were said to be brothers from the community.

"Dem a nuh wrongdoer," a young woman who claimed to know the four men told the Jamaica Observer on Friday.

But the police believe that Bennett, Barrett, and the other two men were involved in the guns for drugs trade with Haiti.

In a release from the Constabulary Communication Network (CCN) yesterday, Bennett o/c 'Guns', was said to have been among a group of men detained by Cuban law enforcers on July 5, 2007.

They were held in Cuban waters with seven 9mm pistols, three revolvers and more than 1,000 rounds of ammunition. The men were said to have been returning from Haiti where they had gone to trade 2,000 lbs of marijuana for weapons and ammunition.

Bennett and the other men were subsequently returned to Jamaica where they were all charged with conspiracy to transport firearms to Jamaica and conspiracy to export marijuana.

The case was subsequently adjourned as the main prosecution witness could not be found to give statements.

Friday's killing — the details of which have not yet been furnished by the CCN — has since been reported to the Independent Commission of Investigations.

Yesterday, Councillor Mitchell said in his experience "nothing like that has ever happened in Black River".

The people, he said, are alleging that "there was no level of mercy" shown by the police. According to Mitchell, the people feel that whatever may have happened the police basically chased the men and killed them.

MY COMMENTS

Most of the information in this report is repetitive to what has already been covered. However, there are a few critical statements that made this report stand out amongst the others. Take note that it begins with the phrase "public anger," which means that the people of that community were displeased with the actions of the JCF. Those officers blatantly abused their authorities and innocent people were killed. This report confirms that the victims were murdered in cold blood, and that the police were shooting indiscriminately. The cruelty was demonstrated in broad daylight, and as the reporter stated, ".... students were on their way home from school." Please note that Councilor Mordant Mitchell said: "Shots were being fired wildly, and anybody could have been hit."

Contrarily, this report states that the police believe Bennett, Barrett, and my brothers were all involved in the illegal trade with Haiti. However, in report 3, the same officers said that it was at least two of the four men who were involved. This is evident of the inconsistencies within these reports. It is confirmed here that the countryside is usually a place of peace.

Notice that Councilor Mordant Mitchell said: "Nothing like that has ever happened in Black River." The Parish of St Elizabeth is among the country areas of Jamaica, where such incidents never happened in a lifetime. As was stated in this report, the surprise attack traumatized the people of the community. The murderers were there to kill anything that was moving. Here it is confirmed that "there was no level of mercy."

CHAPTER 9

WE NEED JUSTICE

"I, A.B., do swear that I will well and truly serve Our Sovereign Lady the Queen, in the office of (here insert the description of the home) without favor or affliction, malice or ill-will and that I will see and cause Her Majesty's Peace to be kept and preserve and that I will prevent, to the utmost of my power, all offences against the same; and that while I shall continue to hold the said office I will, to the best of my skill and knowledge, discharge all the duties thereof faithfully, according to law -So help me God-"

The paragraph above is an oath that every member of the Jamaica Constabulary Force must take before they can sign into office. They must solemnly swear to serve without malice or ill-will, and to ensure that the peace of the Queen is kept and preserved. However, that oath becomes obsolete once those officers get in office. Criminals in Jamaica have a higher chance of being murdered than getting arrested when confronted by the police. An urgent cure is neeed for this life threatening disease. An obvious option is for civilians to defend themselves physically by taking up arms, in fact, that has been done on numerous occasions. However, we all know the results of fighting fire with fire. All out warfare! We have seen from past examples what great trouble war has caused, its detrimental to the economy, the government, and the people. In places like Kingston when the market is forced closed for weeks due to the ongoing crossfire between police and gunmen, far too dangerous for civilians to be outdoors. We have witnessed immense bloodshed and hundreds of dead bodies lying around in the streets. We remember times when the Jamaican government was forced to call upon their allies abroad for reinforcement. Moreover, we understand that we cannot solve a problem of violence with more violence, since that would only erupt a civil war. Therefore, we do not seek revenge, but we are seeking justice! The type of justice that may preserve the lives of the children of our future.

As fired up and as passionate as we were about going all the way to the Supreme Court if necessary, my family did not take the matter to court instantly because of one reason, which is because we were being cautious of the threat that has plagued Jamaicans for decades. To make it plain, police officers will murder you and your entire family if you ever threaten their freedom and position. The fact that most of my closest family members were still living in areas where they were vulnerable to such attacks, unprotected and easily found, made pressing charges immediately, far too risky. Our mother, little sister, Keron, the daughter of Carl, and the son of Kush, were all in unsafe locations. Therefore, the plan was to complete the migration of our family to the U.S., before we began any court proceedings. However, we knew, that alone is a time-consuming process. Anyhow, we chose safety first, regardless of anyone who may judge us because of these precautions. My family could not afford to lose another member, especially while we were still grieving. Therefore, it was critical for us to find safety before we sought justice.

Over the years, crooked cops have become more comfortable with their ruthless activities since they realized that the families of their victims usually chooses to stay quiet. I am quite sure that the ones who murdered my brothers already believe that they have escaped. Nevertheless, we have many unanswered questions. For instance, if my brothers were guilty of the alleged accusations, why were they murdered instead of arrested? What has become of standard police procedures? Like, "...you are under arrest!" Or, "you have the right to remain silent..." The victims of that operation were not even searched. It was d.o.a, dead on arrival!

The first law in Chapter 3 of the Jamaica Constitution states:

"The right to life, liberty and security of the
person and the right not to be deprived
thereof except in the execution of the
sentence of a court in respect of a
criminal offence of which the person has
been convicted."

There are members of the JCF who would rather skip the court and conviction segment and go straight for the kill. People often say that victims of homicides and incarcerations are usually at the wrong place at the wrong time. Well, Kush was murdered in his neighbor's yard, right in the presence of his father. If you are not a wanted man who is on the run, then where can you be safer than in your own home?

Chapter 3 of the Jamaica Constitution also promises:

"Respect for and protection of private and family life, and privacy of the home."

In 2011, the year before my brothers were murdered, a pregnant woman was shot dead because she was cursing a policeman. Those officers have no morals and no respect for anyone, the predicament is spiraling out of control.

Here is another promise of the Constitution:

"The right to enjoy a healthy and productive environment free from the threat of injury or damage from environmental abuse and degradation of the ecological heritage."

Unfortunately, Jamaicans are being denied these rights every day. My brothers were gunned down in the open street while children were walking home from school. Are these types of operations acceptable? That was a question for the Governor General, Sir Patrick Allen. Is it legal for members of the Jamaica Constabulary Force to murder people in cold blood without any form of evidence of a crime committed? Imagine, those same murderers will later join to sing the national anthem, "Jamaica land we love!" It is absolute mockery! How can you love a place but have no respect for the life of its citizens?

Carl and Kush were the strengths of our family, and they were taken away from us very cheaply. Allow me to warn the assassins who were involved in this tragedy that it is not being taken lightly and that we are seeking justice. I will always be passionate about this situation no matter how many years go by. I do hope to see a case or a lawsuit in the courts as soon as possible. We will appeal to the Supreme Court and the Court of Appeals if necessary. I strongly suggest that the Chief Justice, Zalia McCalla, at the time of the incident, and presently, Honorable Mr. Justice Bryan Sykes, take some time out to monitor this ongoing crisis. It is the duty of government officials to demonstrate the most compelling examples of life and liberty. The solution is simple, law enforcement officers who practice police brutality must be held accountable! We wish to see the officers who are comfortable with their immorality obtain a different and a better perspective of authority. Whenever we find success as a nation in this area, then will there be hope for democracy! However, If police officers continue such activities without interruption or fear of penalty, then there will never be peace, and the rule of democracy will continue to be overpowered by bloodshed. Most importantly, we need for every citizen and visitor of Jamaica to become well familiar with their fundamental rights, so that they may stand for them and exercise them daily. After all, the future of the precious island is determined by the decisions that we make today.

EPILOGUE

Kushites is finally released in the year 2023, on the 15th day of December, which is the day when Carl and Kush was buried back in 2012. It has now been 11 years since they were murdered. I began writing this book just a few months after their funeral, when I returned to the United States. The first draft was completed in 2013. At that time, I considered it incomplete. Therefore, I ended it with the words "to be continued," then I saved it and left it alone for a while. My plan was to include the details of what was yet to come. I was really passionate about going to court with the situation, and I wanted this book to include the experience of that journey, including the outcome, and the aftermath.

Now, the obvious question is, what has happened since 2012? The answer is, a lot has happened, but not much pertaining to a court case on the incident. From the beginning, the journey was rather obscure. I spent most of the 11 years assisting my family in the migration procedures, which is now completed, thanks to God. However, it was a long and dragging process. As I stated earlier, 2012 was when I received my permanent resident status. Then, according to immigration policies, I had to wait two years before I was able to file for citizenship, which is the status that is required to invite a relative from overseas. Therefore, in 2015 I became a U.S. citizen, and immediately, I began filing the paperwork for our mother to migrate. Now, that process took another two years to complete, and in 2017 was when our mother first traveled to the United States with an automatic permanent resident status. Sadly, due to certain policies of the immigration process, our little sister wasn't able to travel with mom, even though she was a minor. To make a long story short, as soon as mommy arrived to the U.S. we began filing the paperwork for her daughter to migrate. Well, unfortunately instead of two, that took another five years to complete. The migration process for Ruth was supposed to be completed by 2019, but that was when the Covid-19 pandemic arrived on the scene. The pandemic threw a monkey wrench in the process and slowed everything down, adding another three years to our wait time. Anyhow, in 2022 was when our little sister first traveled to the United States with her permanent resident status. Keron, Dayshawn, and Pretanya are currently in the process of migrating. To include the full details of those 11 years, including the ups and the downs, may be another book by itself. Therefore, I will avoid those details so that we may remain focused on the current topic. Again, we decided not to risk the safety of our remaining family by pressing charges while those murderers were still at large, and most of our family were still in unsafe places. It was a hard pill to swallow indeed, as I watched the years pile up and the chances of justice becoming slimmer.

Nevertheless, in 2018 a part of me lost patience, and I started to do some digging. I began by reaching out to a few people for assistance. I figured the best place to start would be with the lawyer that Callington had hired when he was robbed and beaten in Spanish Town. Thinking that the lawyer would be glad to help once I explained the situation, and that he would even help to identify the ruthless police officers that were involved. Furthermore, I was able to contact Callington's friend, Michael, who was in the car with Carl the day when he was robbed. Fortunately, Michael was on board and willing to help with whatever he could. He said that he was the one who referred the lawyer to my brother after the incident, and that he still kept contact with the lawyer. So far, everything was looking good. I was still in the U.S. at the time, so I asked Michael to arrange a phone conversation for me with the lawyer. He said that it was possible, and that the lawyer's office was not far from his home. However, Michael warned me of a possible skepticism and an unwillingness of the lawyer to go forward digging up an old file. I told him that I understood and that he should proceed anyway. Therefore, the phone meeting was arranged, and the day had come. I was already on the phone with Michael as he walked into the lawyer's office. Naturally, I was expecting something like a formal introduction, but instead, the lawyer was quite discreet. He told Michael to put me on the loudspeaker and let me clarify what it was that I wanted.

"Go ahead, bredda. Talk! He can hear you," said Michael after he pressed the loudspeaker button.

Even though I was displeased with the unfriendliness, I carried on with my pitch, explaining to the lawyer how much suffering it had caused my family to lose my brothers and how passionate I was about seeking justice. I asked him if he would be willing to represent us as our lawyer if we were to take the matter to court. In the politest way that he could, he told me that he was not interested and that he would contact one of his associates who may be willing to help. After the conversation with the lawyer, I thanked Michael for his efforts, but then I realized, that the warning he gave me before the meeting was precise. Most lawyers in Jamaica are afraid to take on a case of such magnitude, because they know that they themselves would be at risk of being murdered. Therefore, there has been no legal penalty nor retribution so far for the cruel actions of those wicked police officers. We have been disappointed since the day of the incident till now, while those ruthless officers are carrying on their legacy.

I challenge the readers of this book to do a little research on the topic of 'police brutality in Jamaica,' then you will see that this plague has affected many more people than my family. I commend organizations like Amnesty International for all its efforts in resolving this crisis. During its Worldwide Campaign Against Torture, a paper was published in 2001 entitled, - "Jamaica: Killings and Violence by Police: How many more Victims?" In 2016, they published a research paper entitled: "Waiting in Vain: Unlawful police killings and Relatives' long struggle for Justice." Then, in 2020 a letter to Prime Minister Andrew Holness entitled, - "Jamaica: Now is the time to legislate to give Jamaica's police oversight mechanism's power to charge and prosecute." There have also been some recent protests in Jamaica following similar, more recent, unlawful killings. I am extremely grateful for each person and each organization who has joined together in the struggle for the pursuit of safety and happiness for Jamaicans. Furthermore, I insist that every government official or person of power play their part in ensuring that justice will be served as we move forward. Even though I migrated, Jamaica is still my native country and the place that I call home, I will always have family ties there. If time allows, I would still like to see a case surrounding my brothers' death in a court of law, and I pray that justice without prejudice will be served. As for my family, we plan to keep an annual memorial celebration in honor of Busky and Kush. Besides that, we will continue the fight against police brutality in Jamaica. This book will be followed by a film documentary surrounding the same crisis, it will include coverage of similar incidents and allow different people to express themselves about the situation. I wish to see the nation moving forward in a positive way, valuing the life of each person.

Miguel Bashford is one the most prolific writers of the 21st century. He proves to be versatile in his contents, with genres ranging from poetry to novels, self help, to real life events. He spent half of his child hood in the challenging environment of Jamaica where he was born, and the other half in Miami, Florida. Miguel is an Amazon best seller, and he is the founder of the book publishing company, Trendstar Publishing. Outside of writing, he is a father, a businessman, and an activist for equality among the races.

www.ingramcontent.com/pod-product-compliance
Lightning Source LLC
Chambersburg PA
CBHW070033040426
42333CB00040B/1667